Contents

'The Little Stranger'

(Above) The Duke of Kent, Victoria's father.

(Below) Queen Victoria arriving at St Paul's Cathedral on her Diamond Jubilee.

On 22 June 1897, millions of people across the world were in party mood. Huge crowds lined the London streets as bands, soldiers and carriages filed past on their way to St Paul's Cathedral. The focus of all this excitement was an old lady dressed in black. She was too stiff even to climb the steps of the cathedral, so the **ceremony** was held outside. Yet this small figure of a woman was the most popular person in the land. To many, she stood for all that was best in Britain. She was, of course, Queen Victoria, and the occasion was the **Diamond Jubilee** of her coronation.

QUEEN
Victoria

Richard Wood

WAYLAND

Titles in the series

Elizabeth I
Henry VIII
James VI/I
Mary Queen of Scots
Queen Victoria
William I

Series editor: Sarah Doughty
Book editor: Joanne Jessop
Consultant: Marilyn Tolhurst
Designer: Jean Wheeler
Production controller: Carol Stevens

This edition published in 1998 by Wayland Publishers Limited
Find Wayland on the Internet at http://www.wayland.co.uk

First published in 1995 by Wayland (Publishers) Ltd
61 Western Road, Hove, East Sussex, BN3 1JD, England

British Library Cataloguing in Publication Data
Wood, Richard
Queen Victoria – (Kings & Queens series)
I. Title II. Series
941.081092

ISBN 0 7502 1910 6

Typeset by Jean Wheeler
Printed and bound in Italy by G. Canale & C. S.p.A.

Cover: A detail from the state portrait of Queen Victoria, 1859.
Frontispiece: The official Diamond Jubilee photograph of Queen Victoria, 1897.

Picture acknowledgements
Archie Miles 20 (top); The British Museum 16; Fine Art Photographic Library Ltd 6, 17 (top); Forbes Magazine Collection, London / Bridgeman Art Library, London 10 (top); Guildhall Art Gallery, Corporation of London / Bridgeman Art Library, London 4 (bottom); House of Lords, Westminster, London / Bridgeman Art Library, London 17 (bottom); Getty Images *frontispiece*, 4(top), 14, 18 (bottom), 19, 23 (bottom), 24 (bottom), 25, 26, 27 (both), 28 (top); The Illustrated London News Picture Library 13 (top), 23 (top); The Mansell Collection 9; Norfolk Museums Service 5, 18 (top), 29 (top); The Royal Archives © 1994 Her Majesty The Queen 13 (bottom), 15 (both), 24 (top); The Royal Collection © 1994 Her Majesty The Queen cover, 7 (both), 8 (both), 10 (bottom), 11, 12, 20 (bottom), 22; Zefa 21. The map on page 28 was supplied by Peter Bull.

During Victorian times, the monarch was the most important person in British society. This 1894 calendar shows Queen Victoria as the head of all aspects of society – the law, the Church, the army and the land.

Few people in the crowd could remember a time before Victoria sat on the throne. If they could, they might have been surprised by all the enthusiasm over her Diamond Jubilee in 1897. In 1819, when Victoria was born, the British monarchy was extremely unpopular. Victoria's grandfather, King George III, had been too old and mentally ill to act as king. His sons, who followed him as George IV and William IV, were also unpopular with the people.

Victoria's father, the Duke of Kent, had been a successful soldier. He died soon after Victoria was born, and the baby princess was brought up by her German mother, also called Victoria, helped by a faithful **governess**, Louise Lehzen.

IMPORTANT DATES

1819 Victoria is born.

1820 The Duke of Kent, Victoria's father, dies.

1830 Victoria learns that she will become queen.

1832 Victoria begins her journal and travels through Britain with her mother.

1837 King William IV dies and Victoria becomes queen.

The baby Princess Victoria with her parents, the Duke and Duchess of Kent.

'The little stranger', as her mother called Victoria, did not have a promising start in life. At first, few people thought that she would ever become queen, so they paid little attention to her. But Victoria's family had great hopes for the young princess. Soon after Victoria's birth, her grandmother wrote that this child was 'destined, perhaps, to play a great part . . . The English like queens.'

As a child, however, Victoria was never treated as an important part of the royal family. 'I was brought up very simply,' she wrote. 'I never had a room to myself till I was nearly grown-up — always slept in my mother's room . . . We lived in a very simple, plain manner.' Victoria was often a lonely child — just once a week another girl came to play. The rest of the time, Victoria played alone with a huge collection of dolls, which her governess helped her to make.

(Above) Victoria's own drawing of her governess, Louise Lehzen.

(Left) Princess Victoria, aged 15, with her mother. Although Victoria as an only child was often lonely, her childhood was not always unhappy. People who met her often said how lively and full of fun she was. She loved dancing, singing and playing the piano; it was said that she had a beautiful singing voice. Victoria was taught at home by tutors and learned to read and write at a young age.

(Above) Princess Victoria, aged 16, with Dash, her favourite spaniel. Victoria was always very fond of animals, especially dogs, and she had many pet spaniels.

Victoria had a great gift for languages, and by her teens she was already fluent in French, German and Italian. Throughout her life she loved to read books of all sorts. She was also a talented artist who loved to draw and paint the people and places she saw. Thanks to her mother, the Duchess of Kent, Victoria received a sound education that prepared her well for her future role as queen.

When Victoria was 11 years old, she learned of her place in the line of succession by studying the royal family tree that her governess had inserted in a history book. It was then that Victoria realized that one day she would be queen. 'I will be good,' was all she said. People knew she meant it, because she was known to be truthful and honest.

(Right) A detail from a painting that shows Victoria being told that her uncle, King William IV, has died and she is now queen.

When she was 13, Victoria set out with her mother on a series of journeys round Britain to see, and be seen by, the people she would rule. She became, perhaps, the first monarch to understand how ordinary people lived. Before the journey, the duchess had handed her a journal to write in. From then until she died, Victoria wrote a detailed and vivid account of every day of her busy life.

Coal miners' houses like the ones Victoria saw during her journey round Britain. She wrote in her journal, 'The country and houses are all black, with wretched huts and ragged children.'

On 20 June 1837, the old King William died, and the pretty 18-year-old Princess Victoria became queen. That night she wrote in her journal, 'I will fulfil my duty towards my country . . . and do what is fit and right.' She never wavered from that promise.

'What is Fit and Right'

(Above) The Archbishop of Canterbury crowning Queen Victoria in Westminster Abbey.

The new young queen was hugely popular throughout Britain. She seemed such a refreshing change from the feeble old kings she followed. However, some people were worried that she was too young and might be easily led by powerful people who had only their own interests at heart. But Victoria knew otherwise. She had a clear idea of right and wrong and could be very **stubborn** with those who disagreed with her. As soon as she became queen, Victoria moved into her own bedroom and then to Buckingham Palace to escape from her mother's influence.

(Right) The young queen's first meeting with her **ministers**.

Victoria's coronation in 1838 was an occasion for great rejoicing. Thousands gathered in London to watch the little queen – she was only 150 cm tall – on her way to Westminster Abbey for the ceremony. Others bought plates, books, medals and pictures as souvenirs of the event. Victoria herself wrote, 'How proud I feel to be the queen of such a nation.'

But there was just one thing missing in Victoria's life: she had no husband to share the burdens of office. Fortunately, she knew of a suitable young man – her German cousin, Prince Albert of Saxe-Coburg.

When Albert visited England in 1839, Victoria immediately fell desperately in love with him. She admired his looks, his intelligence, his charm and his dancing skills. Before long, Victoria proposed to Albert; and Albert's acceptance was, she wrote, 'the happiest moment in my life'. In February 1840, they were married and soon expecting their first child.

IMPORTANT DATES

1838 Victoria is crowned queen in Westminster Abbey.

1840 Victoria marries her cousin Albert; their first child, Vicky, is born.

1842 Victoria and Albert's first visit to Scotland.

1845 Victoria and Albert buy Osborne House.

A detail from a painting showing the marriage of Victoria and Albert. Queen Victoria's white wedding dress set a fashion that many brides still follow today.

The next few years were very happy for Victoria. Of course, her position as queen made any sort of normal family life difficult; but Victoria and Albert were determined not to hand their children over to the care of others, as many rich people did. Victoria's old governess was at first employed as nurse. This did not please Albert, who wanted to control the nursery routine. Before long, Governess Lehzen was sent away and Prince Albert oversaw the running of the nursery.

Victoria and Albert had nine children who were very close together in age. The queen was almost

The royal family in 1843. This was one of Queen Victoria's favourite paintings.

always **pregnant**, and she found this a 'real misery . . . the shadow side' of marriage. Unlike other women, she could not simply withdraw from public life but had to continue with her engagements even when she was heavily pregnant.

Victoria had many royal duties to perform, but she was by nature quite a shy person, and often felt uneasy in the company of **nobility**, **politicians** and bishops. Her solution was to spend as little time as possible at Buckingham Palace and Windsor Castle, the official royal homes.

(Above) The Christmas tree became popular after Prince Albert had one set up at Windsor Castle. This picture of the royal family gathered around their Christmas tree appeared in the Illustrated London News *in 1848.*

(Right) Seven of the royal children presenting 'the Seasons' for their mother in 1854. They are (from left to right) Princess Alice as Spring; Princess Vicky and Prince Arthur as Summer; Princess Helena as the spirit of Empress Helena; Prince Alfred as Autumn; Princess Louise and Prince Albert Edward as Winter. Queen Victoria did not approve of Prince Arthur's bare legs.

Osborne House, the royal family's private home on the Isle of Wight.

Thanks to the rapid spread of railways in the 1840s, it was now possible for the queen to live for part of the year away from London without losing touch with events. In 1845, Queen Victoria bought an estate at Osborne on the Isle of Wight, and Prince Albert, who was a skilful **amateur architect**, set about designing a new country home for the royal family. 'It is impossible to imagine a prettier spot,' wrote Victoria, 'and we can walk about anywhere by ourselves without being followed and mobbed.' However, even at Osborne House, the royal family's privacy was often disturbed by the queen's ministers and government **officials**.

In 1842, on their first visit to Scotland, Victoria and Albert fell in love with the romantic wildness of the 'dear beautiful Highlands'. From 1848 they stayed every autumn in an old castle at Balmoral. They bought the castle in 1852 and later rebuilt it, again to Albert's designs. In Scotland, the royal family enjoyed their greatest happiness. They loved to wear simple Highland clothing, go off for long walks, climbs and picnics, and even stay in disguise in simple country inns.

(Above) A programme for a play performed at Windsor Castle. Actors were often invited to give private performances for the royal family.

(Right) The queen dressed up as a Highland mother with four of her children: (from left to right) Prince Albert Edward, Princess Vicky, Princess Alice, Prince Alfred. When in Scotland, Queen Victoria often wore simple Highland clothes.

'To Play the Queen'

To the public, the queen's life must have seemed very glamorous. Those close to her knew that this was often not so. Every day, wherever she was, dispatch boxes would arrive full of long and complicated papers to read and documents to sign. Throughout her life, Victoria worked very long hours. She needed to understand everything that was going on. In addition, every senior appointment in the army, navy or **civil service** had to be personally signed 'Victoria R' – the R stood for the Latin word *regina* meaning queen. Although she filled any spare moments by 'doing signings', she was sometimes months behind.

IMPORTANT DATES

1851	*The opening of the Great Exhibition.*
1854-6	*The Crimean War*
1855	*Victoria and Albert visit France.*
1856	*Albert given the title* **Prince Consort.**

This 1838 cartoon shows Queen Victoria holding the balance between politicians from different parties. As this cartoon suggests, the queen had a real influence on the government.

Queen Victoria meeting with Benjamin Disraeli, her favourite prime minister. Even prime ministers had to stand in the presence of the queen.

Every week, the queen met the **prime minister** to discuss and advise on government business. These 'audiences' sometimes lasted several hours and could be very difficult if the queen and prime minister did not agree. No wonder the young Victoria once said, 'I do not think myself that it is good fun to play the queen.' Formal occasions could be tiresome, too. **Court rules** forbade anyone to sit down in the queen's presence. People even had to walk away backwards to avoid turning their backs on her.

Despite her small size, Victoria moved with great dignity. People felt a special magic in her presence, and there was never any doubt who was the most important person in the room.

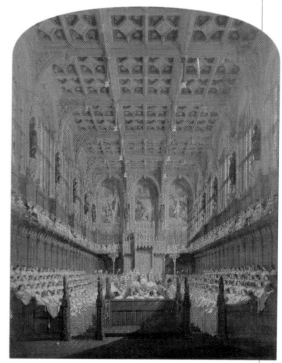

Queen Victoria at a ceremony in the House of Lords. She disliked formal occasions such as this.

Queen Victoria was certainly very energetic. As a young woman, she often danced into the early hours of the morning. Both Victoria and Albert enjoyed going out to the theatre, and they often invited performers to entertain them at home. The queen also loved climbing mountains in Scotland, and even when she was in her seventies could walk several kilometres a day.

Some of Victoria's official duties were a real pleasure for her. One of the most enjoyable was opening of the Great Exhibition of 1851. This vast display of British arts, crafts, science and technology was held at the Crystal Palace in Hyde Park, London.

Queen Victoria's dancing shoes. Victoria was very energetic and loved to dance.

Victoria and Albert at the official opening of the Great Exhibition on 1 May 1851.

It attracted millions of visitors from all over the world. Victoria was especially thrilled because Albert had played a leading role in planning the event. She wrote, 'It was the happiest, proudest day of my life.'

Another high point was the state visit of Victoria and Albert, with their two eldest children, to Paris in 1855. On one occasion, the queen, dressed in plain clothes, took a private drive through the Paris streets to see for herself how ordinary people lived.

Victoria was a naturally kind person who hated suffering. The **Crimean War** particularly distressed her. She called the soldiers 'my own children' and showed them great kindness. The queen was so impressed with Florence Nightingale, who had gone to the Crimea to nurse the soldiers, that she sent her gifts and even invited her to Balmoral Castle.

A photograph of some of the queen's soldiers during the Crimean War. Victoria was upset to hear of the terrible hardships the British soldiers suffered during the war.

'A Nearly Broken Heart'

(Above) Queen Victoria in mourning, photographed with a marble bust of Prince Albert.

The year 1861 was a turning point in Queen Victoria's life. First her mother died and then, in December, Prince Albert died. Victoria was utterly shattered. In twenty years of marriage they had spent only a few days apart. 'My life as a happy one is over!' she wrote. **Widowed** at the age of only 42, Victoria spent the last forty years of her life dressed in sombre black clothes as a sign of **mourning** for the loss of her beloved husband.

(Right) A detail from a painting showing Queen Victoria on one of her frequent visits to Prince Albert's grave at the Frogmore **mausoleum** at Windsor Castle.

The Royal Albert Hall in London was opened by the queen in 1871 as a permanent memorial to Prince Albert.

Albert's death so deeply affected the queen that some people feared for her health. 'They need not to be afraid,' she said. 'I will do my duty.' She meant it. Within a week she was back at her desk signing papers and meeting the prime minister again.

But Victoria saw ceremonies and **social functions** not as duties but as 'extras' to be carried out only when it pleased her. So for many years after Prince Albert's death, Victoria was hardly ever seen in public. Many people lost sympathy with her, and for a time she became very unpopular.

To preserve the memory of Albert, Victoria kept his room at Windsor Castle exactly as it had been before his death. She also carried out Albert's plans to build new arts and science centres in London. The Royal Albert Hall, the Natural History Museum and the Victoria and Albert Museum were all built in memory of Prince Albert.

IMPORTANT DATES

1861 *Prince Albert dies.*

1863 *The marriage of the Prince of Wales and Princess Alexandra.*

1868 *The publication of* Leaves from the Journal of Our Life in the Highlands.

1871 *Queen Victoria opens the Royal Albert Hall in London.*

Gradually, Victoria's terrible grief over the death of Albert lessened. She began to appear occasionally in public. In 1866, she reluctantly agreed to open Parliament, but she refused to wear her crown or robes and made the **Lord Chancellor** read her speech.

The wedding of Queen Victoria's eldest son, Prince Albert Edward, to Princess Alexandra of Denmark in 1863. The queen, still in mourning for Prince Albert, would only watch the ceremony from the balcony and even refused to attend the wedding breakfast.

There were occasional parties, too. Although the queen no longer went out to the theatre or opera, performers came to entertain her at home. In 1870, the famous writer Charles Dickens was invited to Buckingham Palace. Victoria had read his books and shared his concern for **social problems**. The queen was an able writer herself. To keep the memory of

Albert alive she had extracts from her journals published. Her book, *Leaves from the Journal of Our Life in the Highlands*, became a bestseller, and the queen began to regain her popularity.

Without Albert at her side, Victoria sometimes felt lonely and helpless. She could not entirely trust many of the politicians and officials she met at court. Instead, she turned to John Brown, her Highland servant. From 1863, Brown became her closest friend and companion. Victoria respected his blunt speech, honesty and reliability. Some people laughed at this, referring to the queen as 'Mrs Brown'.

(Right) John Brown, Queen Victoria's personal servant, holding the queen's horse at Balmoral Castle.

(Above) An attempt on the queen's life. During her reign, Queen Victoria survived seven attempts to kill her.

The Munshi with the queen. Victoria often worked out of doors in a special tent because she hated hot rooms.

Prime Minister Gladstone speaking in the House of Commons in 1865.

After John Brown's death in 1883, Queen Victoria favoured an Indian servant named Abdul Karim who had been employed to teach her **Hindustani**. He became known as Munshi, which means teacher in Hindustani, and accompanied Victoria everywhere. Unlike everybody else, Karim was very bossy towards the queen. This annoyed her family and ministers, but Victoria always took his side against them. Perhaps she enjoyed being with someone who was not afraid to answer her back for a change.

Victoria's work brought her into regular contact with **diplomats** and government officials. Some, such as Prime Minister Gladstone, she particularly disliked. Gladstone thought the queen was very stubborn, and their meetings were kept as brief as possible.

Prime Minister Disraeli, however, was always a favourite with the queen. Disraeli was also very fond of the queen. He charmed and flattered 'the faery', as he called Queen Victoria, and he once admitted, 'I never deny; I never contradict; I sometimes forget.'

Benjamin Disraeli, Victoria's favourite prime minister, escorts the queen on her visit to his home in 1877.

Victoria had strong likes and dislikes. She was always happier in Scotland than in England. Towards the end of her life she spent over a third of each year in the Highlands. She liked plain talk and plain clothes. She hated warm stuffy rooms and the 'disgusting habit' of smoking. Even royal visitors were forbidden to smoke indoors.

'My Beloved People'

One of the rare photographs that shows the queen smiling. Her smile was described as 'a flash of kindly light beaming from the eyes'.

It is often said that Queen Victoria was 'not amused'. It is true that many later photographs show her looking very glum. But this 'frown' was, in fact, caused by the shape of her cheeks and jaw in old age. People who knew Victoria personally often spoke of her great sense of humour, her laugh, 'the rare beauty of her voice' and especially her sudden and charming smile.

By the 1880s, there was much to smile about. The queen now signed herself 'Victoria RI' for *Regina Imperatrix*, which is Latin for 'Queen and Empress'. Thanks to Prime Minister Disraeli, the queen was given the title **Empress** of India. She took great interest in the peoples of the British **Empire** and enjoyed meeting them. Curry dishes were frequently on the royal menu, and new rooms added to Osborne House were decorated in Indian style.

In June 1887, the whole nation celebrated Queen Victoria's **Golden Jubilee**. The queen had been closely involved in all the preparations; she sent 42 telegrams to the **Lord Chamberlain** in a single day.

(Above) A cartoon showing Disraeli offering Victoria a new crown as Empress of India.

On 21 June, she solemnly processed through the streets, surrounded by kings, queens, princes and princesses from all over the world, many of them related to her. The sadness, **seclusion** and unpopularity of the middle of her reign were now long forgotten.

(Right) Victoria with British, German and Russian royalty. They were all related to her.

By the 1890s, the popularity of the monarchy, and of the queen herself, were greater than ever before. But Victoria's health was failing. She still travelled widely by train and made visits to France as well as to Osborne House and Balmoral Castle. But there were no more long walks, though she still went for daily drives in an open carriage, even when it rained. She did not like people to see her weakness and kept her **bath chair** out of sight.

Queen Victoria's reign had seen great progress. She did what she could to improve the living conditions of the poor, and she welcomed the granting of the right to vote to working men.

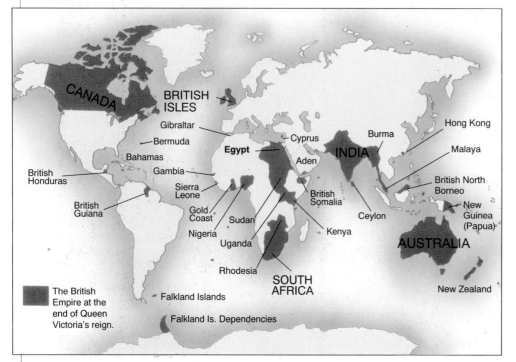

(Above) Four generations of British monarchy. Queen Victoria with her son, grandson and great-grandson, all future kings: Edward VII, George V and Edward VIII.

(Left) A map of the British Empire. During Victoria's reign, so many territories were added to the British Empire that it became the largest empire the world had ever seen.

A Diamond Jubilee cup and saucer. Many people bought souvenirs of special royal events such as the queen's Diamond Jubilee.

Votes for women, however, the queen was strongly opposed to. Her attitude to new inventions varied. She approved of flushing lavatories, and they were installed in all her homes. Telephones she did not like, although she provided them for guests. She also tried out a bicycle, was filmed in moving pictures, and recorded a message on a phonograph record. Motor cars, however, she hated.

By the time of Queen Victoria's death in 1901, life for most of her subjects seemed more comfortable and secure than ever before. In many people's view, the queen, who had reigned throughout the many years of progress and **prosperity**, seemed partly responsible for the benefits they brought, and they loved her for it.

The official Diamond Jubilee photograph of Queen Victoria.

Glossary

amateur Someone who does something as a pastime, not as a profession.

architect Someone who design buildings.

bath chair A type of wheelchair.

ceremony A formal act or ritual that is carried out in a specific way on a special occasion, such as a wedding or the opening of Parliament.

civil service The people who work in government departments.

court rules The rules of behaviour in a royal household.

Crimean War The war fought from 1854 to 1856 between Russia and Turkey for control of the Crimean peninsula in the Black Sea.

Diamond Jubilee The celebration of the sixtieth anniversary of Queen Victoria's accession to the throne.

diplomats Government representatives from another country.

Empire A group of countries or territories under the rule of a single state.

Empress A female ruler of an empire.

Golden Jubilee The celebration of the fiftieth anniversary of Queen Victoria's accession to the throne.

governess A woman who is employed to teach children in their own home.

Hindustani An Indian language.

Lord Chamberlain The head of the management of a royal household.

Lord Chancellor A queen's highest officer.

mausoleum A large, magnificent tomb.

ministers People employed to help the queen carry out her official duties.

mourning The expression of sorrow at the death of someone.

nobility People who belong to a high rank of society and have inherited titles.

officials People who hold positions in the government or some other organization.

politicians People who hold or are seeking to hold positions in government.

pregnant Expecting a baby.

prime minister The chief minister of the government.

prince consort The husband of a reigning queen, who is himself a prince.

prosperity Wealth; success.

seclusion Privacy; hidden from view.

social functions Events at which people gather to enjoy each other's company.

social problems The hardships of ordinary people in society.

stubborn Holding strong opinions and not giving way to others.

widowed Having lost one's husband by death.

Further Information

Books to Read

FOR CHILDREN:
Victoria by D. Turner (Wayland, 1988)
Queen Victoria by D. Shearman (Harrap, 1989)

OTHER BOOKS OF INTEREST:
The Life and Times of Victoria by D. Marshall (Weidenfeld & Nicolson, 1992)
Life on a Royal Estate by M. Tolhurst (English Heritage, 1986)
Queen Victoria by M. Parker (Pitkin, 1991)
Queen Victoria, a Portrait by St Aubin (Sceptre, 1992)
Queen Victoria's Scotland by M. Stead (Cassell, 1992)
Victoria and Albert at Home by T. Whittle (Routledge Kegan Paul, 1980)
Victoria, Portrait of a Queen by R. Mullen & J. Munson (BBC Books, 1987)

Places to Visit

Buckingham Palace, The Mall, London.
Victoria made this her London home. It is still the official residence of the royal family. Open to the public during the summer.

Holyrood House, Edinburgh.
A royal house containing items associated with Queen Victoria.

Museum of London, London Wall, London
Displays include the royal carriage and Victoria's dolls.

Sandringham House, Sandringham, Norfolk.
Queen Victoria bought this house in 1862 for her son Edward, Prince of Wales.

National Railway Museum, York.
Contains the royal trains used by Victoria on her travels.

Osborne House, West Cowes, Isle of Wight.
Favourite family retreat of Queen Victoria, with Swiss cottage and Indian rooms.

Victoria and Albert Museum, Cromwell Road, London.
Opened in memory of Prince Albert, this museum has a fine collection of decorative arts and crafts.

Windsor Castle, Windsor, Berkshire.
Queen Victoria and her family often stayed here.

Index

Figures in **bold** refer to illustrations. Glossary entries are shown by the letter g.